TABLE TENNIS

BROWN

PHYSICAL EDUCATION ACTIVITIES SERIES

Edited by:
AILEENE LOCKHART
University of Southern California
Los Angeles, California

Evaluation Materials Editor:
JANE A. MOTT
Smith College
Northampton, Massachusetts

PHYSICAL EDUCATION
ACTIVITIES SERIES

TABLE TENNIS

MARGARET VARNER
The University of Texas at El Paso

J. RUFFORD HARRISON
International Committee,
United States Table Tennis Association

WM. C. BROWN COMPANY PUBLISHERS
DUBUQUE, IOWA

Manufactured by WM. C. BROWN CO., INC., Dubuque, Iowa
Printed in U. S. A.

Foreword

Margaret Varner and Rufford Harrison, both experts in their fields, have written a most timely and useful book. This first book written on table tennis in the United States in a decade contains a wealth of information on *spin*; it will prove most helpful in all types of ball games where spin and its uses and effects are of the utmost importance. The use of sequence photographs instead of the usual single "still" photos affords the reader a better insight into what can be accomplished.

It is one thing to be able to play a game well. To be able to impart that knowledge and experience to others is a different matter. Both Margaret Varner and Rufford Harrison have proved that they have mastered the art—for it is an art—of passing on their knowledge.

Margaret Varner has represented the United States at the international level in three racket sports—Lawn Tennis, Badminton, and Squash Racquets —and is an expert in racket theory. Rufford Harrison captained the United States table tennis team in the World Championships, is a former president of the United States Table Tennis Association, and is not only a keen student of the game but also an authority.

I wish this book all the success it deserves and know that it will prove helpful to its readers.

Fred Perry
Former World Table Tennis Champion and
Former Wimbledon Lawn Tennis Champion

Preface

Perhaps more than any other sport, table tennis is misconstrued. Although its play under the conditions known by millions is undoubtedly a pleasant pastime, the types of equipment usually used do not permit these players to realize the enjoyment possible when the sport is played well. Yet table tennis is a healthy sport that can be played for all but about the first ten years of one's life. The objective of this book is therefore to show both to a collegiate audience and to players of all ages what table tennis really is, to encourage the use of adequate facilities with good equipment, and to show how one can play the type of game that these conditions permit.

A second objective is to present—probably for the first time in English —the elements of the modern topspin game. Fifteen years after the topspin game was introduced, it is now used by the great majority of the world's top players. Yet in that time, not one book has attempted to present the new style. This book is but an attempt. In the United States, there is limited exposure to modern techniques, and this book certainly cannot cover the fine points. The authors do hope, however, that this basic approach will at least present the fundamentals in the latest style of table tennis.

The authors wish to thank A. Bruce Frederick for the use of the Graph-Check sequence camera; Malcom R. Anderson and Hideki Yamaoka for photographic assistance; and John E. Carr for many valuable comments on the manuscript.

Contents

What Is Table Tennis?

Like other racket sports, table tennis is played between two individual players (singles) or between two pairs of players (doubles). Played well, it demands skill, fast reflexes, top physical condition, and plenty of practice. It is one of the major lifetime sports; once a child is tall enough to execute the strokes fluidly above the table (usually about nine years old), he can begin to learn and can play for the rest of his life.

Table tennis differs from the other racket sports in the magnitude and type of spins employed. The badminton racket imparts no spin to the shuttlecock. A squash ball usually rotates backward, while in lawn tennis forward and backward spins predominate. In table tennis, spin is much more important than in any of these sports; the ball weighs only 2½ grams, and it curves through the air very readily under the influence of spin. The table tennis ball can be made to rotate forward, backward, or sideward, although in the modern game the better players almost all specialize in intense forward spin.

"Ping Pong," a name often heard, is a trade name and is not used to mean table tennis. The term "ping pong" is also used occasionally to mean dull, unenterprising table tennis. Neither use is correct. In the early 1930's, the trade-name owner controlled the sport through the United States Ping Pong Association. In 1933, it was decided that control by one manufacturer was undesirable; the United States Table Tennis Association was formed, and the name of the sport has been Table Tennis ever since.

In an affluent country like the United States, many people have table tennis tables at home, and the less privileged have access to them in community settings. Millions thus play in surroundings that are rarely adequate. A relative few play seriously in table tennis clubs. In contrast, China has ten million registered players; registered players in Japan amount to almost one percent of the entire population; and England has a quarter of a million active players. The International Table Tennis Federation has more affiliated national associations (about 90) than any other comparable body. Table tennis on a world scale is a major sport.

Table tennis is played on a flat table, the dimensions of which are given in Figure 1. This table is centered in an arena that is preferably 46' by 23'. Top players need all of this space. Beginners do not; however, one should at no time play competitively in a room less than thirty feet in the direction of the table nor should the tables be closer together than six feet. Anything less will eventually hamper the game and will ruin

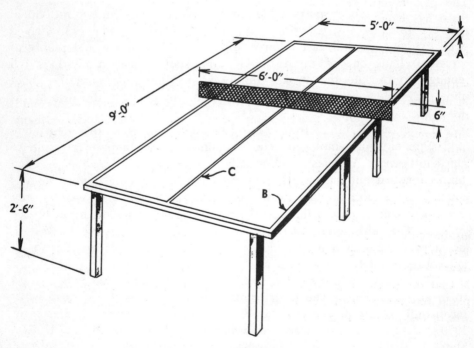

Figure 1—The Table
A usually 3/4", B 1/2-3/4", C 1/8-1/4"

forever a player's chances of development. The ceiling height should be at least twelve feet.

The object is to score twenty-one points before the opponent does. If, however, both players score twenty, then one must win by two points. There are no such scores as deuce or advantage in table tennis although the term Deuce-game is often used when each player wins at least twenty points. There is no such score as an eleven-nil "shut-out."

When the scores are reported, they may be difficult to understand. When Smith d. Jones 3, 22, –19, 20, what actually happened? Mr. Smith won a five-game match in four games, 21-3, 24-22, 19-21, 22-20, Smith's score being given first each time. Note that if the loser's score (e.g. "–19") is reported, the winner's score is obvious. If the eventual winner loses any of the games, the loss is simply indicated by a minus sign.

Matches consist of either two out of three games or three out of five, the latter system being used in individual events in major tournaments. The server at the beginning of one game receives at the beginning of the next; an exception to this in doubles is explained in Chapter 7. The players change ends after each game and also as soon as one of them has won ten points in the third or fifth game, as appropriate. The first service in each game of a match is therefore always from the same end of the table.

The first service is chosen by lot. To serve, the ball is tossed up without spin, and once free of the hand it may be hit by the racket in any way whatsoever. At the time of contact, the ball must be behind the endline. The service must bounce on both sides of the net; subsequent hits, however, must contact only the receiver's side of the table. An otherwise good service that touches the net is termed a let-service and is replayed. Either player can score from any good service by making the other player miss or by making him hit into the net or off the table. Other ways in which a point can be won or lost are discussed in Chapter 7.

Table tennis is an inexpensive sport. A complete set of good-quality equipment, including the table, net, posts, rackets, and balls, can cost less than a hundred dollars. Clothing, on which there are no restrictions apart from its dark, solid colors, is also inexpensive. The main difficulty is that of finding a suitable space in which to play. It is impossible to place too much emphasis on this point: *Do not compromise with the size of the playing area.*

2

Basic Skills

This chapter will introduce all the basic skills necessary to enjoy table tennis. It starts with the modern topspin game, including doubles, and also includes the chop, which was formerly perhaps the most important stroke of the sport. There is much more to table tennis than will be found here, but these basic strokes and tactics are essential before progression can be made to the advanced strokes of Chapter 3 or before the latter will be meaningful.

TOPSPIN

Topspin is so basic in modern table tennis that it is necessary to start with its elementary aerodynamics. In Figure 2, the ball is moving from left to right. At high speed, a layer of high-pressure air, shaded vertically, is forced ahead of it. If the ball has *topspin,* meaning that the top is moving in the direction of the overall motion, friction will carry a thin layer of air around with it. This adds more air above the front of the ball, increasing the pressure in the area shaded horizontally, and it removes air, lowering the pressure, in the diagonally shaded area at the bottom. The net result is that the ball tends to move from the area of dense air to that of light air, i.e., downward.

It is quite impossible to hit a low ball hard onto the far side of the table without topspin. Topspin is absolutely essential to bring the ball down after it has cleared the net. Since if one player does not hit the ball hard, his opponent will, each player must learn to apply this spin. Much of this book is therefore concerned with topspin.

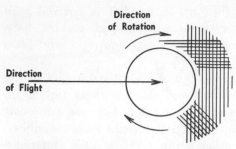

Figure 2—The Effect of Topspin

For two decades beginning in the thirties, table tennis usually featured one player hitting hard with topspin from close to the table, and the other player defending from ten or more feet back. This defensive player would chop down with his racket to apply backspin, which would make it difficult for his opponent to hit. These players all used rackets faced with the pimpled rubber that is familiar to almost everyone. The newer sponge-sandwich rackets (Figure 3) developed in the fifties have made topspin attack against the chop so overwhelming that both pimpled rubber and defensive play are now clearly in the minority. It will be assumed in this book that the student will be using a sponge-sandwich racket. *The descriptions of strokes in this book apply to the sponge-sandwich racket only.*

Figure 3—Different Racket Surfaces

Figure 3 shows three rackets. The one at the left is covered with pimpled rubber, whereas the other two, termed "sponge" rackets, have a layer of sponge rubber next to the plywood. Cork, sandpaper, and plain sponge are not legal.

The sponge racket in the middle of Figure 3 has the pimples in the overlay facing out whereas the one on the right has them turned in; the latter racket has a quite smooth striking surface. For one particular shot (the loop drive which will be introduced last), this *inverted* rubber, as it is called, is essential. For all other shots, there is little difference between the two types; each player should choose a sponge racket simply on the basis of how it feels in his hand.

Topspin shots are almost always made with a *closed* racket, i.e. the top of the racket is closer to the net than is the bottom. Figure 4 shows cross-sections of four rackets. Note that A and B are nearer to the net at the top than at the bottom; they are closed, whereas C and D, with backward slopes, are *open*. A (half closed) and B (slightly closed) are the slopes that will be used most of the time.

FOOTWORK

On almost every shot, the player should turn sideways to some extent and should partly face the ball. Thus for *forehand* strokes—those made by a right-handed player on the right of his body*—the right shoulder and foot should be farther from the table than the left shoulder and

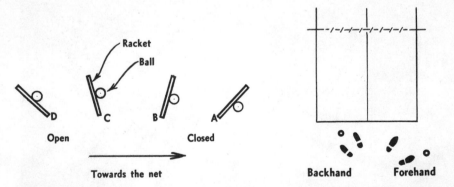

Figure 4—Open and Closed Rackets   Figure 5—Foot Positions

---

*All instructions in this book are written for right-handed players. Left-handed players should make the appropriate changes.

foot. The reverse is true for *backhand* strokes. Figure 5 shows two typical foot positions, with the positions of the ball on contact. These positions are subject to a considerable amount of variation depending on the speed of the ball, its height, the player's position on the previous shot, and the stroke. There is no one right way to do any shot; some ways seem to be better than others for some people, and people are individuals.

THE GRIP

Two basic grips are used in table tennis. Figure 6 shows the orthodox or *shake-hand* grip, used by most players in America and Europe; the forehand side is on the right. To adopt this grip, grasp the racket as if to shake hands with it, allowing the fore finger to slide onto the base of the blade with the thumb on the other side. Grip quite close to the blade, not too tightly. It may be more comfortable to move the thumb further toward the center of the blade on backhand shots, and to do the same with the index finger on forehand shots. Keep these changes to a minimum, however; time is often limited.

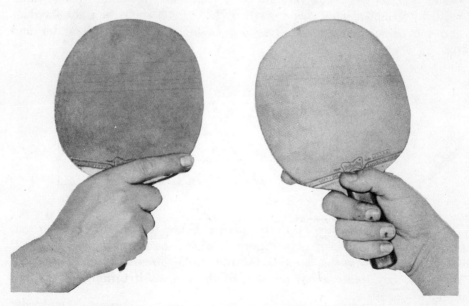

Figure 6—The Orthodox or Shakehand Grip

The other common grip is shown in Figure 7. This is the *penhold* grip, used by most Orientals. The forefinger and thumb reach over the shoulders of the blade, with the remaining fingers spread over the back. The penhold player uses only one face of the racket for all shots whereas the shake-hander uses one side for the forehand shots and the other side for backhand shots.

No one knows which grip is better. This book is limited to shake-hand strokes. For those who wish to use the penhold grip, it is suggested that they remember one simple fact: when almost any stroke is played correctly, the striking surface of the racket moves in exactly the same way as it does when the orthodox grip is used.

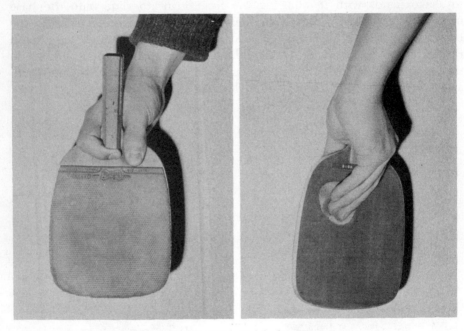

Figure 7—The Penhold Grip

Using the orthodox grip, the player holds the racket straight out from the end of the arm as in Figure 8, which shows the service. Do not bend the wrist from this position for any stroke described in this chapter. The wrist may rotate about the axis of the arm as if turning a key, but it should not bend.

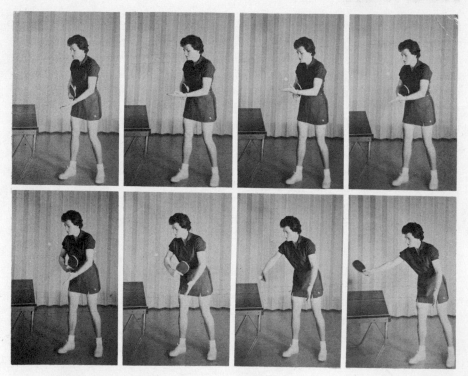

Figure 8—Elementary Backhand Topspin Service

STROKE-PLAY AND TACTICS IN SINGLES

You are now ready to play, with a partner assumed to be another beginner. First, agree on a general principle to be followed throughout practice: you should not both try something new at the same time. While one of you learns a new shot, the other should work with a shot with which he is consistent.

The following paragraphs describe the basic strokes and some of the tactics as used in singles matches.

Elementary Service (Figure 8)—Adopt the backhand stance (Figure 5) with your left foot about two feet behind the end of the centerline. Hold the ball on the flat left palm behind the centerline with your elbow bent almost at a right angle (Figure 8). Toss the ball upward about a foot and catch it. Repeat this until it feels natural. Now hold the racket in front of you, slightly closed and quite near to the body. Toss the ball up again, and this time bring the racket forward slowly to contact the ball as it descends. Let the racket continue forward (*follow through*) after contact. The ball should hit the table near the middle of the centerline at your end of the table, bounce low over the net, and hit again near the middle of the opponent's centerline. The opponent now catches the ball and serves it back: there is no point in his trying to hit it back until you can serve properly to him. The trajectory of this service is shown in Figure 9, Curve 1.

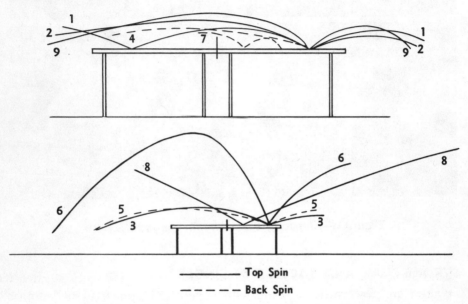

Top Spin

Back Spin

Figure 9—Trajectories of the Various Shots
1 Service, 2 Drive, 3 Defensive Drive, 4 Push, 5 Chop, 6 Lob,
7 Drop Shot, 8 Kill, 9 Loop Drive

If the ball did not bounce on your side, perhaps you failed to close the racket. You may also have moved the racket upward as you hit the ball. The opposite of either of these would result in your hitting too near to your end of the table; the ball could then go into the net or high over it, depending on the speed. If you simply hit the ball too hard, it would probably go off the other end of the table without hitting.

Diagnose your faults in this way if you have no coach: When you have trouble, study your racket angle, direction of stroke, and speed.

The beginner can vary them on this elementary service, attempting to achieve a low ball down the centerline. Your partner can help you by watching your stroke, just as you can help him with his own service.

When you can serve consistently near the centerline, practice serving at different angles. A good player can hit a quarter placed on any part of the other side of the table. You might try aiming first at another racket!

Elementary Backhand Block (Figure 10)—The ball can be returned with almost the same arm action that was used for the service. The opponent serves topspin down the centerline, while you adopt the back-

Figure 10—Elementary Backhand Block

hand stance as if for a service. Contact the ball a few inches after its bounce and, as contact is made, move the slightly closed racket straight forward about six inches. The ball should cross a few inches above the net and bounce on the other side. You can correct your errors as you did for the service; for instance, close the racket less or eliminate a downward motion if the ball hits the net. (An observer or coach will be able to diagnose faults better than you or your partner can.)

A common fault is to hit the ball to one side of the table instead of down the center line. If this occurs, first check whether the wrist is straight. If it is, then change the angle of your feet with respect to the table. Try to put the ball back along the centerline right to your opponent, who should catch it and serve again. As before, he should not try to return the ball until he has some idea where you are going to hit it.

When you can both return the ball in this way, then, and only then, try to keep the rally going. Keep the ball on the centerline at first and

Can you and your partner serve and block using the correct techniques and ball spin? Can you rally three or four times without error along the center line? Then, eight or ten times?

Evaluation Questions

hit slowly. While developing the feel of this shot, you should do little more than let the ball bounce off your racket.

Backhand Drive and Footwork (Figure 11)—When you can block consistently low, you are ready to add speed. The result will be a backhand drive, the first truly attacking shot that will be learned. Still playing down the center, have your opponent continue to block, perhaps from a foot or so farther back than before, while you lengthen the stroke. Start your racket a little earlier and lower—about level with the table surface—and sweep *upward* and across in front of your face. Contact the ball at the height of its bounce or slightly earlier, with the racket slightly closed as for the block. Continue the motion of the racket until

Figure 11—Backhand Drive

the arm is almost outstretched, and keep your eyes on the ball right to the moment of contact.

This last part of the stroke, when the ball and the racket are no longer in contact, obviously does nothing to the ball. The follow-through is nevertheless essential. If you hit hard but stop the stroke immediately after contact, the arm muscles will be tensed at the moment of contact, and you will lose accuracy. It takes less energy to follow through than it does to stop a motion suddenly, and your racket will continue to accelerate right to the moment of contact. Thus, except on a few very specific shots, *always follow through.* The trajectory of a drive is shown in Curve 2 of Figure 9.

The motion of this stroke comes mainly from the elbow, with only a little from the shoulder. At the start, the elbow will normally be about six inches away from the body; at the finish, the arm will be almost outstretched. During the stroke, the player's weight, which is predominantly on the left foot, will shift forward to the right. As the body thus turns slightly, one should get the feeling of carrying the ball on the racket

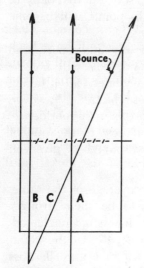

Figure 12—Directions for Backhand Drives

Practicing every shot down the centerline tells both players where to expect the ball, and it enables them to gauge accuracy. There is also a more fundamental reason: The table is shorter in that direction. If you can hit parallel to the length of the table, then it should be no problem to hit diagonally, in the longer dimension.

This is shown in Figure 12. You have already learned to hit down the centerline, at A, where the distance from contact to bounce is about nine feet.* Now, both of you should move toward *your* left sideline and hit the same shot six inches away from it (B). Finally, have your opponent move to the right, while you hit cross court (C). This time, you have a distance of almost ten feet; you can hit your nine-foot shot, and still have one foot of table to spare. It should be easy!

Once the drive in these two basic directions is mastered, players must learn to vary the direction at will. Start by having your opponent move

---

*On this and similar diagrams, the bounce is indicated by a dot on the line of flight.

the ball a foot or so on either side of the centerline, while you attempt to return it to the center with the backhand. This may feel awkward if the feet remain stationary. When the ball bounces to the right of the centerline, the right foot should move a similar amount to the right. When it bounces to the left, the left foot moves correspondingly. This puts your body behind the ball, so that you can make the stroke just like the one already learned. Always *step* to the ball; moving the arm without the foot will result in loss of control.

When you are proficient both at driving and blocking near the centerline, move farther afield, always using the backhand. This calls for more footwork. For a ball that is wide on the right, you will have to move farther onto the right foot, pushing off with the left, and you will probably have to follow with the left foot in order to obtain a comfortable stance. Be sure that you are still standing sideways after this movement. For a ball that is wide to the left, take similar steps with the opposite foot: first the left, then the right. As you do this, stay on the balls of your feet all the time and flex your knees; these two points will become progressively more important as your game progresses.

Practice hitting from any part of the table to any other part, and practice receiving similarly. Using only the backhand, you will not be able to return a ball that is wide on the right immediately after taking one wide on the left. A movement only half way across the table, however, is perfectly reasonable, and you should be able to do this with confidence. Always move the near foot first (the foot that is closest to the line of flight of the ball), and bring the other foot only close enough to give you a balanced stance. Do not cross your legs.

Forehand Service and Block—To complete your coverage of the table, you now need a forehand. Most players find this to be their stronger side; you learned the backhand first to make sure that it was not neglected.

Stand well over toward the left and turn at least 45° to the right, quite close to the table. The foot positions are shown in Figure 5. Toss the ball upward and hit it this time with the forehand side of the racket. Hit just as you did on the backhand—short, horizontally, with a slightly closed racket, down the centerline. There is no need to dwell on this service, since the principles given previously should enable you to correct your errors. Just be sure that you are consistent at serving low down the centerline before you attempt anything more advanced. Then practice forehand blocks just as on the backhand. Start on the centerline, and then learn to cover the entire right half-court. (The forehand

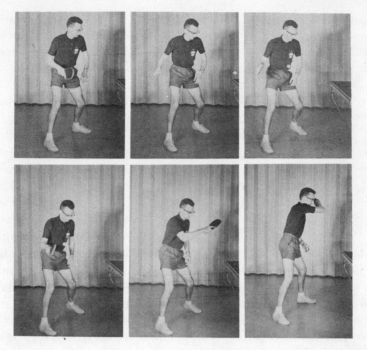

Figure 13—Forehand Drive

block in the left half-court is extremely rare; you need not bother with it at this stage.)

Forehand Drive (Figure 13)—To balance your game, you need an *attacking* shot on the forehand. Serve on the forehand down the center-line and have your opponent block a short distance away from the table. Now, lengthen your stroke as you did for the backhand drive. Start the stroke farther back, with the racket on a level with your right hip; bring the racket *forward* and *upward* as in Figure 13, finishing in front of your head.

Note a fundamental difference between the two drives, occasioned by your physical make-up: As you bring your arm around from the left on a backhand drive, it must finish away from your body, whereas the same arm brought from the right on a forehand will finish either close to your body or just above it. The principle, however, is the same: *Follow through smoothly.* The forehand drive also has more shoulder motion, which makes it the more powerful of the two drives. Watch your op-

What errors are common in executing forehand shots? Can you hit 25 consecutive forehand drives?

ponent do both shots without a ball; you will see that, although he uses his arm in two entirely different ways, the two arcs are almost identical.

Move your weight forward as you hit. Turn slightly from the hips, and bend the body slightly forward. As you hit, the arm should be extended out to the side, with the elbow angle about 135° (i.e. the ball will be about two feet from your body—farther than on the backhand, again for physical reasons).

Ideally, the ball should just skim the net, but you should not aim initially for such precision. If the ball does go as low as that, *lift* more on the upward part of the stroke or else use a less closed racket. You will then have a shot that is virtually as effective as the "ideal," but with more margin for error.

When you can drive consistently, direct the ball crosscourt. Then drive alternately crosscourt and down the line.

Defensive Drives and Footwork (Figure 14)—In the modern game at its best, "defender" is almost synonymous with "loser." Most players therefore attack as much as possible and persist with topspin shots even when driven back from the table.

When you inadvertently present your opponent with a high ball and he obliges with a hard-hit return, retreat. Turn slightly sideways and move back with one foot at a time, just as if you were moving from one side of the table to the other. If your opponent's hard hit is from your left, you will normally expect a crosscourt drive to your right, and you will therefore turn to the right when retreating. Similarly, if you expect him to hit to your left, then make your turn in that direction as you move

Figure 14—Defensive Forehand Drive

back. Be sure you practice these movements, as you will have little time in which to think about them during a match.

When the ball reaches you, perhaps five to eight feet behind the table depending on its speed, perform a shot similar to your regular drive. It won't be quite the same, since the ball will be dropping by the time it reaches you. You will therefore have to *lift* more, and will consequently have to apply more topspin to bring the ball down on the far side. Your follow through should be farther forward than on the normal drive, as in Figure 14. The racket, which should be less closed than usual, will start a good deal lower than on your usual drive, and it will come up more vertically before the follow through. Play the shot fairly slowly until your footwork is automatic—the sooner you return the ball, the quicker you will have to face the music again. The trajectory of the defensive drive is shown in Curve 3 of Figure 9.

For practice, have your opponent drive repeatedly to one part of the table while you retrieve. Then reverse your roles. You will then

What is the neutral position and what factors determine its location? Where should you stand when your opponent is driving from A? from B? from C?

Evaluation Questions
NEUTRAL POSITION

notice that it is harder to drive these balls with their greater amount of topspin; the attacker has to close his racket more in order to prevent the ball from flying over the end of the table.

The principles of the backhand defensive drive are similar to those of the forehand, once you have made allowance for the physical differences explained earlier. Be sure to practice both shots.

Neutral Postion—With a full repertoire of attacking and defensive drives, you must position yourself in order to make the best use of them. During a match, both you and your opponent will force each other out of position, and you will often find yourself at one side of the court rather than in the middle. After you make a shot from any great distance from the centerline, *move immediately* to a position nearer to the middle so that you can reach a ball down the opposite side. Do not, however, return precisely to the centerline. If,

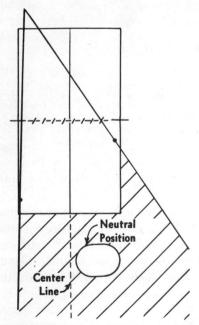

Figure 15—*Neutral Position*

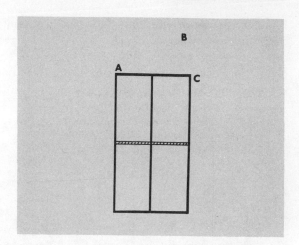

Diagram A:

NEUTRAL POSITION

for instance, your return lands near the far left corner, it will be impossible for your opponent to send the ball out far beyond your left sideline. He can, however, angle wide to the right. In fact, he can control the entire area shaded in Figure 15, so you should stand somewhat to the right of the centerline. Your position will depend on the height of your previous return (if it was high, you should be farther back than usual), on the relative strengths of your forehand and backhand (if your forehand is by far the stronger, then you will stand more to the left, and vice versa), and on what you know about your opponent (if he rarely hits crosscourt, for instance, you will stand more to the left). The position that gives you the best chance of returning safely any possible shot is your *neutral position;* it might þe anywhere in the marked area, or even out of it if any of the factors mentioned is extreme. This neutral position changes after every shot. You should therefore form the habit of moving automatically to the new neutral position immediately after hitting the ball. With this in mind, review pages 14 and 16 on footwork.

The Push (Figure 16)—This lowly-sounding shot, a slow backspin stroke, was the cornerstone of the old drive-and-chop game. The push is now less used, but it still has its place against a ball that is difficult to topspin—a very low, slow ball bouncing close to the net. You risk lifting such a ball too high if you try to topspin it. Backspin is therefore used, so that you can take a longer and therefore more accurate swing.

To apply this backspin, bottomspin, or chop—the names are almost interchangeable—use an *open* racket for the first time. Have your opponent serve or block as short—i.e., close to the net—and as low as he can.

19

First, try a few drives from these balls; if you find it easy to drive fairly hard and low, then your opponent should try to give you balls that are even lower and shorter. When you find them tricky to drive, try the push. Open your racket to about 45°, with the bottom nearer the net than the top, and push it forward under the ball (Figure 16). The racket

Figure 16—Backhand Push

should descend initially and will then move almost parallel to the table surface toward the bottom of the net. Imagine that you are trying to scrape a layer of paint off the table. Take the ball a little later than usual. The whole purpose of this return is to keep the ball low; you are more likely to do this if the ball is not rising when you contact it. Make contact slowly, without wrist. The ball should cross the net low and bounce short (Curve 4 of Figure 9), with a backspin that will at first make your unaccustomed opponent put it in the net.

The most important aspect of this stroke is careful *placement* of the ball. Until the advent of the loop drive, the ideal push landed close to the end of the table in order to limit the opponent's choice of angles. You should still push deep if your opponent cannot loop. Against a looper, however, it will be essential to push short—with the second bounce on the table—to prevent his using his most effective weapon. (The loop drive is responsible for the recent decline in the use of the push; the loop drive is a difficult shot, which will be discussed in the next chapter.)

Most players have no backhand loop and many have weak backhand attacks. Most pushes are therefore aimed at the backhand, but many players make the mistake of pushing that way exclusively. Avoid that error. The push is a tactical stroke, and judicious use of angles can force the opponent into error. Practice pushing *to all parts of the table.*

Your opponent, meanwhile, is probably experiencing trouble since he has not met backspin before. If your pushes are low and short, he will have to push in return. If not, however, he should drive, and this is where he will have trouble. Unless he uses a less closed racket, he will probably hit the net. Any ball with backspin can be driven, but this requires a less closed racket and more *lift* in the initial part of the stroke. The follow-through will finish somewhat higher than usual.

A common error in pushing is trying to apply an extreme amount of spin to prevent the other player from driving. This idea is not as good as it sounds. Although spin is used on almost all shots because it provides control, the effort necessary to apply extreme spin will have the opposite effect—and on the push, control is of the essence.

Another error is to return the ball too high. This could result from hitting too early—a natural error in view of your previous stress on early contact—or omitting the downward part of the stroke at the beginning. With all of these points under control, you should be able to produce a sound return. Many players neglect footwork on this shot, since a central position enables them to reach almost anything without moving. It cannot be stressed enough, however, that a well-controlled shot is more likely to result if you are in position; avoid taking any two pushes without moving your feet between them. Move the near foot toward the ball on each push. Be on the balls of your feet all the time; since a loose return could be hit hard, you may have to retreat rapidly. And be sure to turn toward the ball.

You will find the forehand push less comfortable than the backhand, and most players try to avoid it as much as they can. That does not alter the fact that the forehand push is essential to your repertoire. An error that is common on the backhand and even more so on the forehand is following through across the body; be sure that the follow through is toward the net. This will give you much more control.

The Chop (Figures 17 and 18)—The chop used to be one of the principal strokes of table tennis, but topspin has lessened its importance considerably. The chop is an extension of the push, and the loop drive therefore makes it almost a liability. Nevertheless, some players are psychologically suited to a defensive game—and there is nothing like a chop for putting a player on the defensive.

Although the push and the chop are both backspin shots, they are different. The push is a sparring shot; the chop is one hundred per cent defensive, although a good defender uses it tactically. Figure 17 shows a forehand chop. It is taken about as far back as a defensive drive but, as in the push, the racket is open. Turn sideways and start with a slightly open racket, somewhat lower than the shoulder and a little behind the body. Bring the racket downward and forward in an arc, and hit under the ball when it is roughly level with your right leg. Follow through almost horizontally. The ball should return a few inches over the net, and land near the endline—Curve 5 in Figure 9. You cannot make it land near the net unless its trajectory is high, and a high trajectory near the net invites a fast, angled return. Chops should therefore be deep, even at the risk of a loop drive return.

Probably the most common error in chopping is hitting too soon, in which case the racket is in front of your body as you hit. In this position, the ball will be descending at a less steep angle, and your return will rise too high, thus offering your opponent an easy drive. Be sure to wait and take the ball from your side.

Figure 17—Forehand Chop

Another common error is to attempt to load up the backspin. Avoid any wrist motion whatever until you have good consistency; otherwise steadiness will always elude you.* Concentrate instead on keeping the ball low by taking it well to the side.

In this connection, most top international defenders do not use sponge rackets, which apply the most spin, but instead use plain pimpled rubber. On the pimpled-rubber racket, the vicious spins applied by attackers have less effect, and the defender can control them more readily. Control is much more important than extreme spin. If you decide to defend and to change to pimpled rubber, you will have to modify your strokes. Lack of space permits no detail, but you should bear in mind that the entire stroke with "rubber" is more vertical, including the follow-through. The shot is described well in other books—see page 71.

The backhand chop (Figure 18) must be taken closer to the body and is often made with the racket, at the time of contact, vertically beneath and only slightly forward of the head. This graphically illustrates

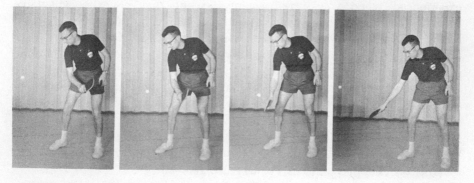

Figure 18—Backhand Chop

what is true for every good stroke, forehand or backhand, attacking or defensive: The body should be inclined in the direction of the ball. On the backhand chop, you are even more likely to make the mistake of hitting in front of the body. The only time you do this is when the ball is aimed directly at your body and you have no time to move. Even

---

*As you improve your consistency, you will find it possible to increase the spin by opening the racket far more than is shown in Figure 17, and wrist motion will be unnecessary.

Which of these racket angles is suitable for the chop? Which other shots require the same angle?

Evaluation Questions
THE CHOP

then, take the ball as late as possible by leaning forward; this will move your waist back, and you will have more room to stroke.

When you chop, your opponent will have the same trouble that he experienced when you were pushing, except that now he will have plenty of room for a backswing. At no time should he push your chopped ball if its bounce takes it beyond the table. A less closed racket than usual, probably with a more vertical swing, should enable him to continue driving with no further difficulty.

A good chopper can give an attacker a considerable amount of trouble. If you reach that stage, you will find that you can put plenty of spin on one ball, and next to none on the next. Or you can return several balls with little spin, and then one that is "loaded." The methods for doing this are outside the scope of this book, although some of the remarks on chopped services (p. 34) are relevant.

TACTICS IN DOUBLES

Unlike the other racket sports, table tennis prescribes that the two partners on a team must hit alternately. Furthermore, the service is permitted only from the forehand court diagonally across the table, a ball landing on the centerline being considered to be good. The International Table Tennis Federation recently permitted the service to begin beyond the extension of the sideline. In doubles, the server can therefore stand to the right and leave the entire space behind the table open for his partner. Until you have learned the advanced services described in Chapter 3, however, it is advisable to serve from fairly close, where you can be confident of serving safely. Emphasize the backhand. If you are right-

Diagram B:

THE CHOP

handed, your use of the backhand when serving and receiving will give your partner plenty of room; it will, however, put you well away from your neutral position, and you will have to concentrate more on moving there after your shot. If you are left-handed, you have a great advantage in doubles since you can use your strong forehand and still keep out of your partner's way.

Theoretically, the game of doubles is just like singles; position yourself for the shot, and execute it just as you have already learned. The problem is that it is not so easy to get into position; you are not quite sure what your partner did on his last shot, and it is always possible that he may be in your way. For this reason, most good doubles players move out to one side immediately after hitting the ball, and then they move back behind the neutral position as soon as possible. After hitting hard, you will find it easier to move aside in the direction of your follow-through. If your shot is not hard and you have little bodily momentum, you should simply move to the nearer side.

Figure 19 shows a typical sequence. In the left diagram, partner A hits a hard drive, while B is approaching the neutral position from his previous shot. A's follow-through takes him to the left from where you see him, in the center figure, moving to his neutral position. The return from A's shot comes to B's backhand. B therefore moves to the left to hit this ball and, since the ball is at the left side of the table, he continues in that direction after the shot. The return from this shot (last figure) is driven fairly hard as A moves in from the left. A, who has a strong backhand, uses it as he moves over. He continues to the right, leaving the table open for B, who is coming in from the left. A could have approached

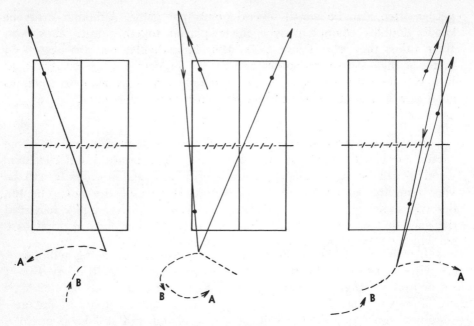

Figure 19—Typical Sequence in Doubles

the same ball with his forehand, in which case his follow-through may have taken him to the left.

Your opponents will be much more out of position in doubles than in singles, and it is obviously advantageous if you can drive hard when they are thus partly incapacitated. But beware! You may be in the same trouble. Do not attempt to hit hard when you are out of position. A champion may do that, but it will require considerably more practice before you can. Instead, a slow deliberate shot, nicely placed, can be just as effective as a hard drive, and it may be much easier to control. This does not mean that you should never hit hard in doubles—it means that you should build up to your hard hit with good placement, patience, and care.

In addition to watching the ball and your opponent, you should also observe your partner as he makes his stroke. By knowing what he does to the ball, you can better anticipate the return. His body motion will tell you which direction he is likely to take after his shot. Good rapport between you and your partner, which can result only from playing together often, can be worth several points per game. Although everyone knows doubles champions who never played together until they won their titles, they also know pairs who, individually, can be beaten by many of their defeated doubles opponents. Rapport is a great advantage. If it can help these players, it can also help others. A team is never so good that it cannot benefit from a few extra points per game.

* * *

You have now been exposed to all the basic strokes and to some tactics employed in table tennis. Your game should be fluid and consistent —and it will be if you have practiced each shot assiduously. It will be very tempting to try the more glamorous strokes of the next chapter, but you should resist the temptation until you have thoroughly mastered the ones that you have already learned. You will then have a good base on which to build a more advanced and powerful game.

3

Advanced Strokes

In this chapter, you will learn some advanced versions of shots that you already know, and you will also be exposed to some new shots. Many of these require the utmost control, and you will have to practice each one religiously. If you proceed gradually, learning one shot at a time, there is no reason why you should not master them all.

THE KILL (Figures 20 and 21)

The kill, "put away," or smash—the hard-hit ball that supposedly cannot be returned—is to many the most satisfying stroke in table tennis. Many beginners therefore overdo it, which is why the shot was not introduced earlier. Many players who have learned the feel of the kill attempt it too often and too early, thereby frequently missing what should be a point-winner. You must be able to drive repeatedly, working your opponent from side to side and from back to front, until he makes an error. Only then should you kill, and then only when truly in position. Be patient; it is far better to win on the twentieth hit than to miss on the second.

In the chop-and-drive days, one heard a lot about the "flat" kill, and you should still learn it for use against a chopper. When presented with a short, chopped ball about a foot higher than the net, move your racket horizontally, with the blade vertical, and hit very hard with plenty of follow-through. Since the ball is high, you need not worry about its backspin finding the net; once the ball has changed direction, the backspin becomes topspin and will bring the ball down. The stroke is known as

28

the flat kill since no lift or spin is added by brushing up on the ball. Be sure to turn sideways and take the ball well away from the body, preferably with the forehand. On balls that are close to the net, you may hit too far to the side if you fail to turn sideways, and the ball may miss the table completely. Follow through with your body as well as your arm; at the end of the stroke, your body should be facing the table or perhaps be even to the left.

Against topspin, the flat kill will send the ball off the end of the table. In this case, you must hit above the ball as on a drive. You need not, however, lift the ball, so that the first part of the normal drive stroke can be dispensed with, i.e., you can flatten the backswing: Swing the racket more or less horizontally (even downward if the ball is particularly high), keep it half closed (Figure 4A), and hit hard. Experience will dictate to what degree the racket should be closed; you should close it as little as possible in order to put as much direct force into the shot as you can, but it will always be necessary to close it to some extent. The stroke is shown in Figure 20, and its trajectory in Curve 8 of Figure 9.

Figure 20—Forehand Kill

These kills are not supposed to be returned. You can therefore afford to put every bit of your body into it and *really* follow through. Use a full arm stroke reasonably far from the body. On the forehand kill, your weight will come forward more than on a drive, and you may have to move your left foot farther forward during the stroke to maintain your balance. You must be limber in arm, body, and legs. Follow through across your body as far as is necessary to hit the ball really hard—*and then return immediately to your neutral position.* Although the shot is not meant to come back, an occasional opponent will not have read that part of the book. Never assume that a point is won until the ball is dead.

Figure 21—Backhand Kill

The backhand kill (Figure 21) is a difficult shot that many players—even internationals—try to avoid. It is physically impossible to put as much body into the shot as on the forehand. Use the forehand kill as much as possible but develop the backhand as an extra weapon.

THE LOB (Figure 22)

It was hinted above that you can return a kill, and so you can. You must, however, return it safely; your opponent must be disarmed as much as possible, and you must give yourself as much time as you can to prepare for his next onslaught. One answer is the lob, the essential ingredients of which are *depth,* to prevent an angled return; *topspin* and often *sidespin,* to make the return more difficult to judge; and *height,* to give you more time and to reduce the possibility of a drop shot. (See Curve 6 of Figure 9). Height will also cause your opponent to expend energy in hitting downward as well as forward. A high topspin ball cannot be killed as readily as one at

Figure 22—Forehand Lob

medium height. In addition, the shot should usually be directed to the opponent's deep backhand, since the backhand kill is difficult.

Being an answer to the kill, the lob is always taken at a considerable distance from the table, usually ten feet or more. By this time, the ball is probably descending. In order to *lift* it with the right amount of topspin, the racket must be approximately vertical and only a foot or two from the floor. A slightly open racket is easiest for learning, but as you perfect the lob, close the racket slightly and add more spin.

On the forehand, the racket will usually start behind your right leg. Bring it upward, following through more vertically than usual and finishing the stroke over your head. Allow for the height and speed of the kill, and try to land the ball, after a trajectory that takes it about twelve feet from the floor, within a foot of the backhand corner. On the backhand, the shot begins in front of the rear leg, with the forearm almost touching the front leg; the follow-through is in front and to the right of the head.

Common faults in the lob are insufficient topspin and unintentional sidespin. Lack of topspin results from too open a racket. It is natural to think that, in order to lift the ball high, the racket must be underneath it. This is not true. A slightly closed racket will lift the ball, and only a closed racket will provide enough spin to reduce the effectiveness of the next kill.

Sidespin is inadvertently applied by stroking slightly in front of the body instead of to your side. It can be a valuable adjunct to the lob, but not until you have had much more practice. Turn sideways!

Implicit in this discussion of the lob is the assumption that you can reach the ball. When practicing, your partner can hit to a part of the table decided by mutual agreement, but in a match you will have to rely on anticipation, which comes only with experience. Don't be disappointed if you cannot reach all the kills; it is, after all, your opponent's purpose to prevent you from doing that. In time, you will find yourself returning more and more. Your anticipation will improve if you watch your opponent's body motion in addition to that of his racket.

Later on, when you can anticipate better and can return a good percentage of your opponent's kills, try making life more difficult for him by adding wrist motion to the lob. Drag the wrist, i.e. hold the hand nearer the floor than usual until contact, at which time you can snap it quickly in the direction of the follow-through. This will add more topspin; the amount can be varied with the amount of wrist. Avoid trying this until you are consistently returning kills.

The lob looks easy to hit against, but actually you are fairly safe. If your opponent tries to drop shot from the endline, you will have ample time to run to the table. He will therefore probably attempt another kill. If he hits early or late, he will need perfect timing in order to avoid error. He is therefore most likely to hit at the height of the bounce; the ball will have farther to travel, and you will have more time.

When you are attacking against the lob, concentrate on hitting at the height of the bounce from above the ball, without applying spin. Hit hard, and, on this one shot, hit short so that the ball will rebound high and possibly out of reach at the other end (Figure 23). As you do this, watch the bounce very carefully, for if it has sidespin the ball could go out beyond your racket.

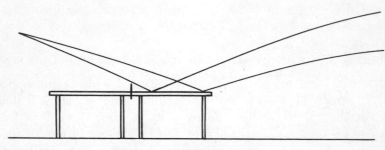

Figure 23—Killing the Lob

SERVICES

The service is restricted as described on page 59. The sponge racket can nevertheless give such an advantage to the server that if you fail to make use of this advantage, you will penalize yourself to the extent of several points per game. Advanced services were not introduced earlier, to ensure that you would first develop a versatile, patient, and consistent game. Far too many players learn one good service, only to have their games degenerate into a series of attempted serve-and-kill-the-return sequences, many of which do not work. Not every service will put you in command; if one does not, then you must be prepared to use all the shots that you have already learned. Many types of service should be learned and used at random, so that your opponents will not become accustomed to any of them. Furthermore, you should reserve one or two particularly effective services for the crucial stages of your matches. Some types of service are described in the following paragraphs.

Topspin—You have already learned this service. Now, you should practice varying the speed and spin. A slow service with plenty of topspin, performed by using more wrist than usual, is quite effective when mixed with fast services.

Where is the best place to contact the ball to return the lob shown in this figure? What method of stroking and what spin do you recommend?

Evaluation Questions

RETURN OF LOB

Most backhand topspin services are directed wide at the opponent's backhand, usually his weaker side. (Figure 24, Line A). He will therefore not expect the ball B, to his stronger side. A third type, C, a fast ball directed to his right hip, forces him to decide whether to use his forehand or backhand; his indecision can result in a poor stroke, but only if your service is fast. Another variant, D, is a very short, slow service bouncing very close to the sideline and passing over it rather than over the endline; it forces your opponent to negotiate his way past the right corner of the table. Try it; it isn't easy.

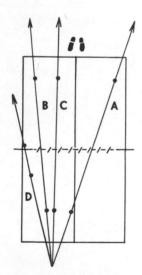

Figure 24—Placement of Backhand Services

Forehand counterparts of these services are less common, but are effective if used sparingly.

Chopped Services—A chopped service should usually be short; otherwise, it invites a loop-drive return (p. 42), especially if it is expected. The deep chop can be effective to the backhand, but be sparing in using it elsewhere. These services are performed just like a chop, except that the point of contact is higher.

Skill in these services lies in disguising the amount of backspin, which can be done by adding wrist motion. One can move the arm fast with a stiff wrist, or hardly move the arm at all while snapping the wrist, and produce exactly the same amount of backspin. Alternatively, a service with a short arm motion can have con-

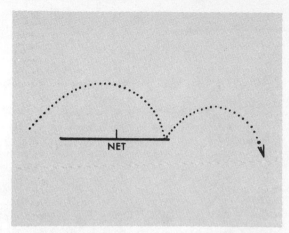

Diagram C:
RETURN OF LOB

NET

siderably more chop than one with a long backswing and follow-through. There is little point in all of this attempted subterfuge if your opponent knows exactly what you are doing; you must keep him guessing by making the stroke almost horizontal. The motion will be almost in the direction of his eyes, so that he is less able to gauge the lengths of the different components of the stroke. As you vary the amount of wrist, be sure also to vary the amount of arm motion. Being more noticeable than wrist motion, it will tend to distract your opponent's attention.

Disguised Topspin and Chopped Services—One way to make it difficult for your opponent to know which spin is on the ball is to use perspective. As in the previous example, bring the racket up to the ball horizontally. If it is slightly closed, you will apply a slight topspin; conversely, a slightly open racket will apply chop. It does not matter that only slight spin will be imparted, if the opponent cannot identify it. Lack of perspective on the horizontal stroke will make identification difficult, especially if you add a sidespin.

Rapid vertical motion will also confuse the issue. When you toss up the ball in service, bring your racket vertically downward with the blade vertical. When it reaches the ball, lift it again immediately, all in one very rapid motion. Hit the ball either just before or just after the lowest part of the swing. If you do this rapidly enough, your opponent will be unable to tell whether you made contact on the down stroke or on the up stroke.*

---

*At the time of writing, this service is perfectly legal. Some players, however, have made this and related services so devastating that the ITTF is considering outlawing them.

Sidespin—You can make the ball rotate about a vertical axis by brushing it horizontally with a vertical racket. Figure 25 shows one example

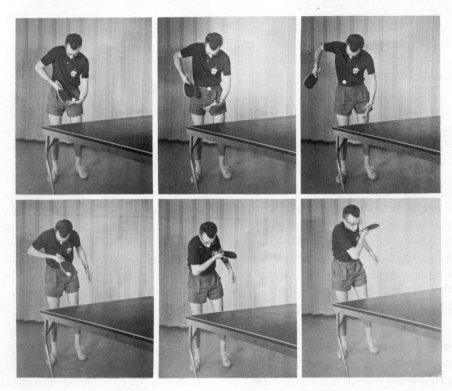

Figure 25—Sidespin Forehand Service

of such a service, with the racket handle above the blade. Another method is to crouch with your left knee almost on the floor and hit forward on the right of the ball with the racket handle pointing down; this will produce a spin in the opposite direction to the one shown in Figure 25. In many services, you will have to contort your body quite differently from your usual stance.

You can also apply sidespin about a horizontal axis parallel to the sideline. Hold the racket with its blade vertical and perpendicular to the net with the handle pointing toward you, and strike downward and slightly forward. The top of the ball will rotate to the right, and the ball will tend to break to the right when it hits the table.

Combinations—Pure sidespins are rare, but the mechanics of producing them should be remembered in order to combine them with topspin and backspin. These combinations are as difficult to describe as they are effective. In any case, they are out of place in an introductory book. You will do much better to devote time to perfecting your strokes rather than to working out services that will win the point outright. Nevertheless, a few experiments will provide an interesting break in your practice. You don't even need an opponent for service practice.

To surprise the opposition, it is quite tempting to rush the service. Resist the temptation! With all the variation that is possible, it is easy to miss a serve completely. Make a point of holding the ball quite stationary on your palm for at least one second, and during that time think very deliberately about what you are going to do.

When you deliver a deceptive service, you should try to do it in a way that is, to you, predictable; i.e. you should know what your opponent is likely to do with it, so that you can anticipate his return. This means that you must move in a particular direction to kill what you hope will be a loose return. Before making this movement, wait until your opponent's move is irrevocable, so that he cannot change his mind. Derive as much advantage as possible from your services.

RETURN OF SERVICE

When learning the service described in Chapter 2, you returned it with a simple block. With all the variation that you now know is possible on the service, however, the return can obviously be difficult to master. Yet this is clearly one of the most important aspects of table tennis. The cardinal rule is to watch your opponent's racket meticulously. Do not watch his arm motion; nor his shoulders (which often tell you where his drives are going, but which are valueless as an indicator on services); nor his eyes; nor the height to which he throws the ball. *Watch his racket.* Analyze the topspin or bottomspin, the sidespin, and the speed.

If the sidespin is imparted by a vertical motion, you can almost ignore it. Its purpose is largely to confuse you and to cause an unusual bounce, but it will have no other effect unless the racket is very closed or very open. On the other hand, if the ball is spinning around a vertical axis, take care. If the racket in service moves from left to right, as in Figure 26, so will the ball when you return it; your opponent is attempting to make you angle the ball, possibly off the right side of the table. You must therefore angle the racket correspondingly in the opposite direction—toward where the opponent's racket started.

When is sidespin used and for what purpose?

Evaluation Questions

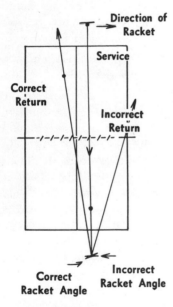

Figure 26—Angles in
Return of Service

If the service is chopped, the safest return is a push underneath, to prevent your return from hitting the net. The more effective return, of course, is a drive, but it is more dangerous since you will have trouble gauging the amount of backspin on the ball.

A topspin serve can also be returned by either stroke; you will usually find the drive to be quite safe if you apply enough topspin of your own to bring the ball down.

If you are in doubt, as you may be on many services, push deliberately high and prepare yourself for a hard-hit return. Remember, however, that you are now playing directly into your opponent's hands; time spent in learning to return lower balls will pay dividends.

When returning the service, stand so as to favor your best stroke. Be on your toes, with your knees flexed and ready to move in any direction. If your opponent rushes the service and delivers it before you are ready, don't try to hit it; you have the right to indicate that you are not ready. One object of the rules is to prevent you from being rushed when still recovering from the previous rally.

Evaluation Questions

How do you judge the amount and kind of spin when receiving a serve? What must you do to return the topspin, chop, and sidespin services?

THE DROP SHOT

The drop shot, a short delicate shot played when a drive is expected, was a powerful weapon in the days of the chop. It is less useful now as more players adopt the topspin game, but you will still find it invaluable whenever you meet a chopper.

In the middle of an attacking rally, when your opponent is near the barrier (see p. 15), suddenly check one of your drives in mid-swing; open your racket, and just let the ball bounce off it over the net. A good drop shot should bounce twice on the table. A little backspin will help to shorten the distance between bounces, and the shot should be aimed at the centerline near the net. If it is not near the centerline, there is risk that the ball will cross a sideline before bouncing again. The time between two bounces on the table is about half a second. If, however, the ball can drop to the floor (Figure 27), your opponent will have roughly twice this time in which to reach it—and a fit player can cover the necessary ten or fifteen feet in one second with a couple of long

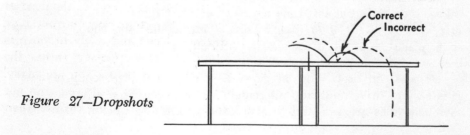

Figure 27—Dropshots

Which oncoming ball permits the use of a loop drive and why? In making a loop drive, where should you contact the ball after the bounce and with what racket angle?

Evaluation Questions
THE LOOP DRIVE
(See p. 42)

steps. So keep the drop shot short. Many players have trouble doing that. Their shots go too high or too far, largely because of too firm a grip. It is often necessary to relax the grip deliberately, so that the racket is virtually "dead."

Another error is in "dropping" the wrong ball. For the best effect, the chopped return should itself be low and near the net. If not, your drop shot will have farther to go before crossing the net, and your opponent will have more time. You may tire him, but you won't prevent him from reaching the ball.

If your opponent is out of position, you may make an exception to the suggestion that the drop shot be on the centerline. A shot over the opponent's distant sideline can, in that case, obviously be effective.

Your drop shots will lose much of their value if you fail to disguise them. You *must* take the backswing like a drive—actually start the drive motion—before slowing the racket for the drop. In this way, you will ·catch your opponent on the wrong foot, and it will take him longer to reach the table.

Against topspin, you must change much of this. You should still select a low, short ball, but this time your racket must remain closed, and your grip must be even looser than when playing against the chop. The drop shot against topspin is extremely difficult, and unless you are truly ambitious you may well ignore it.

A word on drop shots in general: Don't let them become a habit. It is easy to drive and drop alternately, or on some fixed schedule, since such schedules are essential to avoid short rallies in practice. You must

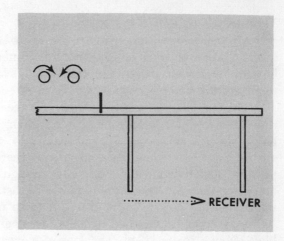

Diagram D:

THE LOOP DRIVE

RECEIVER

make a conscious effort to avoid letting this pattern become a match-play habit. Your opponent can analyze such habits and therefore can anticipate all your drop shots, thus destroying their effectiveness.

THE BLOCK OR HALF-VOLLEY

The next shot that you attempted after the service was a half-volley, and it was not a very ambitious affair. You used it only very briefly since other strokes were more effective. There is, however, a time and place for everything. You have little choice but to half-volley when close to the table and faced with a sudden hard hit, but this is a matter of desperation. The half-volley can also be used quite deliberately to change the pace of the game. Either use requires a great deal of anticipation, which you did not possess when you were first learning.

When you half-volley, *follow through*. You did not do this with your original half-volley; the follow-through is the distinguishing feature of the more advanced version. Start the shot exactly as you learned it originally, with a closed racket near to the bounce of the ball; take no backswing, but follow through just as on a drive. This follow-through will give more authority and greater control; it will convert a passive stroke into an aggressive topspin weapon. Practice blocking—half-volleying—both cross-court and down the line while your opponent drives as hard as possible from whatever distance you both find necessary for consistency. Be sure to take no backswing. It is the lack of backswing that distinguishes the half-volley from the drive. If you develop the habit of using a backswing, you will have insufficient time to execute the shot in a hard-fought game.

41

THE LOOP DRIVE (Figure 29)

All budding topspin players aspire to this difficult shot, which is used against a chopper or against a topspinner's pushes. Before learning it, be sure that your drives and kills are consistent. Without a good kill, there is little point in looping.

The loop drive is simply a shot with excessive topspin. The idea behind a drive is to put a lot of energy into moving the ball across the net, and only as much as needed is converted into spin to bring the ball down on the other side. Now, imagine instead that you put as much energy as possible into topspin and add only enough forward motion to get the ball over the net. The result will be devastating when the ball reaches the opponent's racket, where it will tend to rise vertically. A good looped ball may never be returned to the table at all; if it is, it will probably be high enough to be killed. The loop drive can be played effectively only on a chopped ball. Your topspin adds to the spin already on the chop, so that the looped ball rotates with the sum of both spins. If the oncoming ball has topspin, that will destroy some of the spin resulting from your stroke. The loop drive is therefore a weapon for use against backspin. You will find it more effective if you use inverted rubber.

All this spin is brought about by skimming the ball tangentially with the racket. Compare the idealized cross sections of a ball and a racket at impact during a drive (Figure 28A) and during a loop drive (Figure 28B). To skim the moving ball very fast like this is extremely difficult. Few players can pick up the loop drive at their first attempt. If you cannot, you will have to approach the shot gradually.

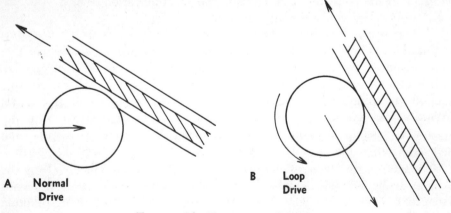

A   Normal Drive   B   Loop Drive

Figure 28—Drives at Impact

As shown in Figure 29, the ball is struck when descending. Swing upward vertically with a vertical racket, to contact the ball perhaps two feet from the floor. If the impact sounds much like a drive, then the ball is sinking too far into the rubber and it will probably go off the

Figure 29—Forehand Loop Drive

end of the table. Now close the racket slightly, listening to the sound all the time, and move the swing slightly forward. As you do this, the impact will become almost inaudible. If you miss the ball entirely, you will know that you have gone too far.

Some coaches recommend doing this early practice alone. Drop the ball at arm's length from about six feet above the floor. As it descends from its bounce, try to skim it over to the other side of the table, pivoting from the waist upward. When you are applying a good spin, you will

43

hear very little sound, and the ball will bound forward rapidly on hitting the table. You are then ready to try playing again with a partner.

In your early practice, your opponent should, of course, always chop to the same part of the table, but later you will have to learn to move rapidly to get into position. Be very agile in order to keep the ball at arm's length as much as possible, thus adding more spin.

To help your practice, your opponent should chop back your loop to maintain backspin on the ball. This will be difficult unless he retreats until the ball is almost on the floor. By chopping almost horizontally with a quite open racket, it will be possible to return the ball fairly low, and you can continue to loop.

As your opponent is learning this defense, you will be presented with plenty of high balls. Beware! The chopped loop will be the hardest chop that you have ever encountered, and the ball will never even reach the net if you try to kill it in a normal fashion. A less closed racket ought to be the answer, but most players find that a fairly closed racket, played forward almost horizontally, yields the most consistent results.

As on the lob, many players inadvertently loop with sidespin. Most opponents soon adjust to this, so that it is well worth while to develop the correct stroke. The error stems from the natural urge to hit at the height of the bounce. If you wait until the ball is dropping at your side, you will hit with pure topspin.

For a topspin player, the best defense against the loop drive is of course a topspin return. If you can topspin the loop consistently, you need not be afraid of the opponent who loops your pushes. The easy way is simply with a variant of your regular drive: Close the racket so that it is almost flat on top of the ball and drive slowly with a more horizontal motion. If this sends the ball off the table, make the stroke lower, and close the racket still more. As your confidence increases, you will be able to add to the speed of the return, thus permitting you to regain the attack almost immediately.

There are many variations of the loop drive that are out of place here: combinations with sidespin, slow and fast shots, and backhand loops. Try them by all means—but not until you have mastered the standard forehand loop. There are also many modifications of the other shots previously learned. Some are discussed in the reference materials listed on page 71, and others are described from time to time in table tennis periodicals.

4

How To Progress

Progress comes with practice, fitness, and experience. This chapter covers the first two of these.

PRACTICE

Practice should include stroke play, footwork, strategy, and match play. Unfortunately, most players ignore the first three and simply play games. In a game, one tries to win, and one concentrates on the strokes at which one excels. It is therefore good to make a general rule: play games only after your practice session. Routine practice may be boring if not done with some imagination, but it is quite essential.

Practice one shot at a time for about half an hour, and be sure that both you and your opponent have a complete understanding of what you are both trying to do. If he is a match-play-only man and will not practice, then find someone who will. Practice all versions of a shot. For instance, you might start by hitting crosscourt drives for ten minutes and see how many you can hit in succession. Then hit down the line for ten minutes and alternate for ten minutes.

In such practice, include a different shot occasionally to keep the other player on his toes. Be sure to try to return all net and edge shots. Nets and edges are impossible to practice, yet during a table-tennis lifetime you will be faced with thousands of these shots. The more you can return, the more points you will save. It is safest to return a bad net ball with a push.

With the side of the table against a wall or arranged as in the illustration, how many returns can you make in 30 seconds? With the vertical surface divided into sixths, can you hit each target on eight out of ten tries? Can you do it from progressively greater distances from the wall?

Evaluation Questions
STROKE PRACTICE

Practice hitting only with the backhand or only with the forehand, while your opponent moves you around. This difficult and tiring practice is excellent for footwork and reflexes.

You can improve your footwork and the fluidity of your strokes by practicing against a wall. Topspin to a point about six feet up the wall, and let the ball bounce before repeating the shot. Start your wall practice with the backhand, which is usually neglected in this exercise. "Target practice" will help your consistency; try aiming between chalk lines. Practice drop shots with a line about six inches from the net. Lines a similar distance from the ends and sides are useful for drive practice, but remember the center of the table, too. Shots placed there unexpectedly can be very effective, and many a better player has trouble handling a hard hit to his body.

Footwork—Footwork is often neglected, since there is much more glamor attached to the arm stroke. Practice moving from side to side and retreating and returning to the table. Be sure that you lead with the near foot before moving the other. The oft quoted rule about never crossing the legs may have to be broken occasionally, but when you do, always ask yourself if you really had to do so.

Be sure to *keep your eye on the ball* until the moment of contact. Then immediately watch your opponent until he hits the ball. Watching his backswing, shoulder motion, and racket will help you to anticipate his return.

General Suggestions—When you are consistent with all your strokes— and only then—experiment with a little *wrist* motion, especially on the

Diagram E:
STROKE PRACTICE

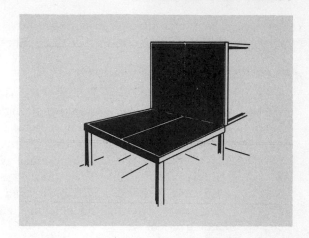

push; top players constantly vary the amount of backspin and sidespin on this shot. Spin variation on lobs and loops is also valuable.

Practice occasionally when you are aware of being tired. Many coaches recommend stopping when tired, lest further play damage your stroke pattern. In a tournament, however, it is often necessary to play when tired, and you must be able to keep going. When tired, you may have to decrease the speed of the game to give yourself more breathing space. Play from a little farther back, and spin more or push if you find your drives losing accuracy. To do this well in a tournament, you must have practiced it first. If you have a coach, be sure he is watching and knows that you are tired. It is very easy to develop unconscious faults, which he can bring to your attention for correction. The drive tends to become shorter and jerky, yet even a tired player can follow through smoothly if he concentrates. The racket tends to become slightly open, and footwork gives way to too much reaching. Such habits are quite difficult to correct if permitted to become set.

If you have a coach, then you should tactfully pay little attention to anyone else. Perfectly good advice can conflict with your coach's equally wise counsel. Any shot can be played in an infinite number of ways; if someone suggests a new way, be sure to check with your coach.

If you have no coach, you will have to copy other players—but do not copy the strokes of a pimpled-rubber player unless you too have that type of racket. Select the best strokes from different players. When you do experiment, give everything a fair trial, whether it be a new racket, a stroke, a practice drill, or anything else. Change rackets, by all means. But *you* or your coach should be the judge of what is right for you, not some top player with perhaps an entirely different game. Having changed rackets, give the new one at least a three-month trial before rejecting it.

EXERCISE

Table tennis demands physical fitness, which suitable exercises will help you achieve. Any sort of exercise for strength and stamina will suffice. Circuit training (see Robert P. Sorani's book in this series) has recently found great popularity among the European and Asian coaches; select exercises that strengthen the legs, arms, and waist. The Royal Canadian Air Force program, obtainable from most news stands, is also helpful. Exercise of this sort is useful only if performed regularly. It involves only a few minutes per session and can be done daily by even the busiest of people. Do not overlook it.

In addition to these exercises for strength and stamina, warm-up exercises are also valuable. They are not essential for practice, since the practice itself will serve this purpose. (It can, however, be dangerous to start practice with vigorous play; work up to it gradually.) In a match, you should not start cold. The body is never as productive when cold, and you cannot afford to let a warm opponent build up a lead while you loosen up. A few minutes of jogging will serve fairly well, though some top players use very detailed warm-up exercises. At least one world champion precedes each match with enough warm-up exercise to make him perspire.

5

Patterns of Play

Knowing the strokes and knowing when to use them are not the same. Opponents rarely play like practice partners. They come in various styles, each with its own strengths and weaknesses. Contrary to a common tenet, do not overplay these weaknesses. Repeated shots at your opponent's weakness may serve as practice for him, and the weakness may disappear before the end of the match. Furthermore, working at this weakness may mean working your own. The Chinese strategist, Hsu, says, *Play to your own strength.* It is sound advice; reserve your opponent's weakness for special treatment in an emergency.

TACTICS IN SINGLES

Singles tactics can best be considered in terms of the various stereotyped styles of play adopted by most players. These styles of play are discussed in the following paragraphs.

The All-Out Hitter—This is what you are probably aiming to be, so you must immediately face one fact: If the other player is the better hitter, you will probably lose. There will be little point in your trying to stay close to the table and hit quicker than he can. You must find a different solution. There are several ways of reducing your chances of defeat. First, of course, as in playing against almost any opponent, use your services to get on the attack before he does. If one service is working particularly well, however, don't overdo it. You must not permit your opponent to get used to your best weapon. Try to reserve one good service for the end of a tight game. In general, keep your services low, stress backspin and sidespin, and remember your shots down the line.

When lobbing, vary the spin in the hope of forcing your opponent to miss. When his hit comes exactly as anticipated, return it with a sudden hard drive. (Remember to close your racket more on this *counterdrive* than on your previous lob.) The element of surprise may cause your opponent to yield a weak return, which should permit you to grasp the initiative. Approach the table quickly after a counterdrive.

If you are desperate, try a little subterfuge. Suppose you are obviously going to lose the first game. Then try a few balls that you know your opponent likes. Don't be too obvious about it, but nevertheless let him have a good time. Some players in this situation will become over-confident, losing their timing after a few of their best shots. Your chances of success will then be vastly greater.

Usually you will want to move your opponent around as much as possible. Make him work hard. If you are fit, perhaps you can defeat a technically superior player in a different manner: Outlast him with your greater stamina.

The Blocker—The man who half-volleys virtually everything returns the ball before you can recover from your follow-through. He is an exasperating type who fortunately seems to be disappearing. Since you cannot hope to be quicker than he is, treat him like the hitter. Keep the ball deep so that he loses the advantage of acutely angled returns. You may have to stand farther from the table than usual to give yourself more time. In fact, take all the time that you need, since blockers with very short swings by necessity are usually not hard hitters. Vary the spin and, for safety, try lifting the ball more than usual; blockers are often more at home with low balls than they are with what you would consider to be the perfect ball to hit.

You can also try a few lobs, which are even more difficult for the average blocker. And, of course, make full use of your services, although the blocker can probably handle them fairly well.

The Chopper and the Pimpled-Rubber Player—These are classed together, since pimpled-rubber players are usually defensive.

A consistent chopper seems to return everything while apparently permitting you to control the game. Since you want to attack, his play should be exactly what you are looking for—if you do not fall into a common trap. When an opponent chops back four or five balls in succession, many hitters become impatient and begin to hit harder in an attempt to clinch the point. This is precisely what the chopper wants. The ball that you decide to hit harder may be the one that he has chopped less—and so it disappears beyond the endline. The key to winning against the chopper is *patience*. Be willing to drive ten or twenty times while looking for an opening. Mix your drives with drop shots. Loop drive if you can, and you should have no further trouble. Cover the entire table with randomly placed shots, the loops being directed largely to his backhand.

In addition, vary the pace. After a series of hard drives a slow drive is often more effective than a drop shot. Since it looks like a drive, your opponent will stay deep and will then have to lunge to the slower ball; when a player lunges, he usually hits high. Finally, remember a weakness common to players of all types—their middle. Angle most of your drives, but also hit a few directly at your opponent.

You will meet a few players who use pimpled rubber, which applies less spin than sponge, and you will tend to hit their chops off the table. You must therefore close the racket more and hit farther forward. (On the other hand, if the rubber man is hitting, there will be less topspin than usual for you to overcome; you will therefore close the racket *less*.) Furthermore, your own spin will "take" less on the opposing racket—which is why the international choppers use rubber. You may therefore have to wait longer before getting a loose return from your drives and loops. *Be patient*.

The Spinner—Spinners are often defensive players, but they do not rely so much on straight-forward chop. Their specialties are exaggerated sidespins and topspins, mixed with occasional heavy—and light!—pushes. Watch the opposing racket and the bounce of the ball very carefully so that you can compensate for the spin. These spinners are often one-ball hitters; they vary their "stuff" until you yield a loose return, which they efficiently kill. You must avoid this loose return if at all possible, although against a more conventional player it may often be quite safe.

Make an attacking stroke whenever you can. Loops will give you the chance to kill. Drives will keep your opponent farther back, thus dissipating his spin before it reaches you. Avoid trying his fancy spins; it is too late to learn that device in a match. Concentrate on more orthodox spins and on your own strong points.

TACTICS IN DOUBLES

Individual doubles opponents can be handled as described for singles, but they must nevertheless also be treated as a team. Move them as much as possible. An occasional hit directly at the player who just returned the ball is often quite effective. Services are almost as valuable as in singles, but your own partner may not know exactly what you are doing. A Japanese trick is helpful here: By means of hand signals under the table immediately before serving, the Japanese tell their partners exactly what is coming so that they can position themselves accordingly. Without this understanding, watch your partner's racket closely when he is serving.

You cannot hit everything in doubles, since you will often be out of position. The byword, *patience*, is even more important in doubles than in singles. Instead of trying to blast everything, try to force your opponents into a weak return so that your partner can kill. The good doubles player manipulates the play to the extent of forcing the opponents to set up a return that can be killed *by his partner*. This is particularly important in mixed doubles. Given the opportunity, most women can kill very competently, but the man has the better ball control; it is he who usually furnishes the loose balls for his partner to hit. As Johnny Leach, twice world champion, says, "Play to your partner's strength." For instance, there is little point in looping if your partner cannot handle the return. But if he has an excellent backhand, a judicious use of sidespin may effectively put the returns where he can do the most with them.

TEMPERAMENT

You can be a good player even if you have a poor temperament—but you will never be a *great* player. It is therefore worth spending some time in eliminating your rough spots, and the earlier the better.

In Individual Play—The most important factor is to ignore the score. Whether you are leading 1-0, 20-11, or 23-22, or losing 11-19, play the point as if the match depended on it. With a comfortable lead, concentrate; *don't* take it easy. Once you relax the pace, it becomes remarkably difficult to put the pressure on again. Games have been lost from 20-11, and yours could be the next. Ignore the fact that, at 19-17, you need "only" two points. Points come one at a time, and that is the way to play them, mentally as well as physically.

When you make a mistake that costs you a point, analyze what you did wrong and promptly proceed to the next point. Brooding about that last point, even if it was the potential match winner at 20-19 in the fifth, may cause you to lose the next. Convince your opponent that all is serene at your end. If he realizes that you are worried, his confidence may increase; on the other hand, your own confidence could make him erratic.

Finally, display no bursts of temper. The player who slaps his thigh—or the table—with his racket, the man who throws his racket when he loses, the one who curses when he misses a shot—these are players who are destined to keep losing.

In Team Play—A good team player must be able to forget his individual record. If you are overly worried by an individual loss, you should not be playing for a team. Even losses can help. If you play a long match and lose, your opponent may be so weakened that he will lose to your teammates, whom he would perhaps normally defeat. So forget your loss, and determine to win the next encounter. Your time is much better spent in encouraging your teammates than in commiserating with yourself.

The Language and Lore of Table Tennis

Much of the language of table tennis can be understood quite clearly from the preceding chapters. Some possible points of confusion are explained in the following paragraphs.

RACKET, PADDLE, BAT

These synonyms are, respectively, the official, the U.S., and the English terms. The official term is gaining ground rapidly in the United States.

RUBBER, SPONGE, SANDWICH

Many players restrict the word *rubber* to mean pimpled rubber. Furthermore, since pure sponge was made illegal in 1959, sponge means any of the sandwich coverings (p. 5). If the pimples of the overlay face outward, the sponge is *regular*; if they face inward, it is *inverted* or *smooth*. Pimpled rubber, which enables players to chop and defend from long distances from the table, made table tennis a major sport in Europe in the 1930's. Two decades later, sponge led to the modern topspin game in the Orient.

THE SCORE

See page 3. The server's score is always called first, even if he is losing at the time.

RALLY, POINT, LET

A *rally* is an entire play from service until the ball is dead. If it is scored, it is a *point*. If it is not scored for any reason, it is a *let* and is replayed. "Let" is simply an old English word meaning a hindrance. The word "let" is heard, not "net," when a service hits the net.

GAME, SET, MATCH, TIE

These terms are not standard. When you win 21 points, you usually win a *game*, although some call it a set. A group of games, e.g. two out of three, constitutes a *match*, although this also is sometimes called a set. An encounter between two teams is termed a *tie* or a *team match*.

DEFAULT, WALK-OVER, RETIRE

Often confused, these terms are precise. A *default* is a penalty whereby the disciplined player is not permitted to play a scheduled match. Typical reasons include late appearance, illegal clothing, and unbecoming conduct. The defaulted player's opponent receives a *walk-over*. This term, derived from horse racing, is used more in other countries; in the United States, "default" is often confused with it. A player who cannot play may elect to *retire*, and his opponent, too, receives a walk-over. Players retiring without good reason have been found guilty of unbecoming conduct.

RACKET HAND

A player may not hold a racket in each hand. A very few players switch hands in mid-point, but there is no time for this in a heated game.

COURT, ARENA

These are synonyms for the area enclosed by the barriers surrounding the table. These barriers, usually about 2′6″ high, do not confine the players, who are at liberty to vault over them if they wish. (A player who leaves the court for any reason other than to play the ball, however, will get a black look from the umpire. "Play shall be continuous.") The term "court" also means a player's half of the table.

VOLLEY, HALF-VOLLEY

To *volley* the ball is to hit it before it bounces; it is always illegal. (See p. 60). A *half-volley* is a legal shot made immediately after the bounce.

DOUBLE BOUNCE, DOUBLE HIT

These are self-descriptive, and both are illegal. The *double bounce*, sometimes termed "not up," occurs most often after a drop shot. A *double hit* can occur at any time.

COUNTERDRIVE

Other shots have been described in Chapters 2 and 3. The *counterdrive*, however, needs some clarification. It is simply a drive of a drive and was originally used by a chopper to upset a hitter's timing. Whereas it was formerly played from some distance behind the table, in the faster topspin game it can be made from any distance. You have met it in several guises: The half-volley and the defensive drive are both counterdrives.

DEEP, SHORT

A ball bouncing near the endline is said to be *deep;* one near the net is *short*.

LOOSE

A *loose* return unintentionally gives the opponent an opportunity to attack. A push that is too high and a loop drive with insufficient spin are both loose returns.

LOADED, DEAD, HEAVY

A *dead* ball carries virtually no spin. The opposite, a ball carrying as much spin as can be imparted, is said to be *loaded*. A loaded chop is *heavy*.

EXPEDITE AND TIME-LIMIT RULES

Two choppers with excellent defenses and mediocre attacks pushed for two hours in the 1937 World Championships before one scored a point. In a women's singles final, pushing went on for so long that the title was declared vacant. The ITTF eliminated such endless matches by means of the *time-limit rule*: Whichever player was leading after twenty minutes was declared the winner. If the score was tied at this time, the players were given five minutes for one more point, and both were defaulted if no point was scored. This rule shortened some matches, but it did nothing to eliminate dull pushing. The United States adopted the *expedite rule*, which replaced the time-limit rule universally in 1963. If any game lasts longer than fifteen minutes, the serves alternate, and the receiver automatically wins the point if he can return thirteen hits. Once applied, the rule stays in force for the rest of the match. It is obviously expedient for the server to attack, thus adding interest to the game.

SLOW, FAST

A *slow* table appears to retard the progress of a drive, and defenders therefore have more time to reach the ball. Conversely, a *fast* table is favored by attackers. A *fast* racket is more resilient and imparts more speed to the ball than a *slow* racket.

UMPIRE, REFEREE

As in lawn tennis, the *umpire* is in charge of the match. The *referee* is in charge of the entire event; appeals are made to him on points of law.

OPEN AND CLOSED TOURNAMENTS

Only players from a limited geographical area are eligible for a *closed* tournament. Conversely, anyone may play in an *open* tournament. Unlike some other sports, table tennis makes virtually no distinction between an amateur and a professional; the term "open" has nothing whatever to do with this problem.

DRAW, BYE, SEED, PLACE

The playing schedule of a tournament, showing who plays against whom, and what happens to the winners, is termed the *draw*. (See Figure 32.) Players who advance to the second round without playing in the first (p. 67) are said to receive a *bye*. Players who are strong enough to justify separation from other strong players are *seeded;* a *placed* player is given similar though somewhat less favorable treatment.

WORLD CHAMPIONSHIPS

Since the ITTF has no amateur regulations, table tennis is not an Olympic sport. Its world champions are decided biennially at a tournament with seven main events: the men's and women's team championships (Swaythling and Corbillon Cups respectively), men's and women's singles and doubles, and mixed doubles. Lady Swaythling and M. Marcel Corbillon were among the pioneers of the International Table Tennis Federation.

7

Laws of the Game

Following is a simplified version of the laws published by the United States Table Tennis Association:

EQUIPMENT

Table tennis equipment is described in Chapters 1 and 9.

THE TOSS

The game starts with the toss of a coin. The winning player (or pair) may elect to serve or to receive first, to begin play at one particular end, or to request the opponent to make the first choice. The other player then makes the remaining choice. In doubles, the serving pair then determines the first server, and finally the other pair selects the receiver. Many pairs desire to select the starting order; they therefore receive first if they have that choice.

THE ORDER

Players change ends after every game, but the first service in each game is always from the same end. The first pair to serve in any doubles game selects which partner will serve, but then the receivers must play so as to reverse the order of the previous game. If A served to X in the first game, then X must start by serving to A in the second, or else his partner (Y) will serve to A's partner (B). Since partners must hit alternately, the order in the first game would be AXBYA . . . , and the second would start XAYBX . . . or YBXAY. . . . In the last possible game of a match, the players change ends as soon as one scores ten points; in doubles, the receivers change their order of receiving.

THE SERVICE

The entire free hand must be flat and horizontal, with the fingers together and the thumb spread out. The ball rests on the palm from where it is tossed upward. The service must be visible to the umpire. As Figure 8 shows, this rule is simpler than it sounds. It originated in the late 1930's when U. S. players developed finger-spin serves that even top internationals could not return.

The players in turn deliver groups of five services. In doubles, the players serve in the order described above; the receiver always serves the next group of five serves. If the score reaches 20-20, or if the expedite rule (Chapter 6) is in force, the service alternates after every point instead of after every five.

Once tossed up, the ball must be struck behind the endline or its imaginary extensions.* It must hit the table before and after crossing the net. The server wins the point if a served ball bounces twice in the receiver's court; he is under no obligation, as many beginners believe, to ensure that the second bounce is off the table. In doubles, the service is diagonal, starting from the right half-court. Services hitting the center-line are good.

EDGE BALLS

A ball that hits the edge of the table is good. (Figure 30.) A ball clearly hitting the side, however, is not good. If the ball crosses over part of the table before hitting, it obviously cannot hit the side and must therefore be good. If it hits from outside the table, its bounce will suggest whether it hit the edge or the side.

WRONG ORDER

If the wrong player serves or if a player serves from the wrong end, the error is ignored if not discovered until the end of the game. If it is discovered sooner, play continues with the order appropriate to the score that has been reached as if no mistake had been made. All points already scored are counted.

---

*This and the rule calling for the order to change in each game in doubles will be reconsidered by the ITTF in 1967.

GOOD RETURN

A player makes a good return by hitting the ball, after its bounce on his court, directly to the other side. It may touch the net or the post and may go over, around, or under the extensions of the net beyond the table. A ball hitting the racket hand is considered to have struck the racket.

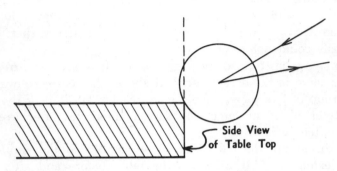

Figure 30—An Edge Ball

LET

The umpire calls a let, and no point is scored, if (a) the served ball touches the net or post and is otherwise good or is volleyed, (b) the ball is served before the receiver is ready, or (c) there is any external influence on the game. If the receiver wishes to claim that he was not ready, he must not attempt to hit the ball. There is no limit to the number of let services.

A. LOST POINT

A player loses a point if he misses the ball completely or otherwise fails to make a good service or return. In addition, the following are all illegal while the ball is in play: moving the table, touching the net or post by the player or his effects, volleying the ball, returning the ball with an empty hand, and touching the playing surface with the free hand. Furthermore, a player may not touch the ball with his body or effects while it is over the table. The volley, however, is illegal even if the ball is clearly behind the table; this strange rule was introduced when there were many half-volley players, who habitually stand very close to the table.

IN PLAY

The ball is in play from the toss of the service until it touches either a racket or the table twice without touching anything else in between or until it touches something else. If the ball bounces back to the previous hitter because of intense backspin, the receiver may run around the net to hit it.

SCORING

The first player to acquire 21 points wins the game, except that he must win by at least two points.

DISCONTINUOUS PLAY

Play is continuous except for unusual circumstances and for an optional five-minute rest after the third game of a five-game match which must be taken at the request of either player. Short breaks are permitted if a player damages his equipment or becomes ill. When an illness is due to the strain of play, however, the umpire may refuse the rest if he believes that it would adversely affect the other player; a table tennis player should be fit.

DRESS

Apart from the shoes and socks, which are perferably white, all other garments must be of dark, solid colors.

COACHING

Players may be coached during a match only when its continuity would not thereby be affected.

8

Unwritten Rules

Unwritten rules make up tradition, and there is little tradition in a young sport like table tennis. There are, however, common courtesies such as are found in any sport. For instance, it is a courtesy to everyone present to dress well. It is a courtesy to other players not to intrude on their courts and not to raise your voice or otherwise interfere. And it is a courtesy to your opponent to behave decorously and fairly.

When playing in a club, be sure to have your own supply of balls; players who habitually use other people's balls are not welcomed. Offer to keep the score if there is no umpire, and offer to do your bit in the work of the club, especially in setting up and dismantling equipment.

In a tournament, introduce yourself to any opponent whom you have not met. Warm up seriously, making sure that all have the opportunity to practice all shots. Refrain from using the allotted two minutes for your complete warm-up, however, which should have been done on a practice table. After the match, be sincere in your comments: if you lost, admit it without excuses. Give your opponent a warm handshake, and thank the umpire for his services.

If the tournament regulations call for losers to umpire, do so willingly and gracefully. You welcome a good umpire for your own matches; try to be one yourself. All players should know how to umpire; the United States Table Tennis Association has a manual on the subject and a test-paper for those who wish to qualify.

Some players always annoy the tournament committee with requests for information. Keep your requests to a minimum; the committee will do a better job without them. If your entry was refused because of lateness, withhold your complaint; just resolve to enter earlier next time.

The cardinal rule in all this is quite simple: Be a model to others. If you are, no further time need be spent on unwritten rules.

9

Equipment

Good table tennis demands good equipment. Although the sport is inexpensive, stores seldom carry much equipment of good quality. Many stores limit their stocks to complete sets, often incorrectly labeled "Official" and often hopelessly poor. Some criteria of good equipment are listed below. If such material is not available locally, ask at your local club; you can obtain its address from the local sports editor. If there is no club, write to the USTTA (see p. 72).

BALLS

Look for the USTTA seal of approval and the legend "USTTA Approved." If in doubt about quality, two easy tests will eliminate most inferior balls: Check for soft spots by squeezing between finger and thumb, and look for wobble by spinning on a smooth surface. Good balls may be available locally at about twenty-five cents each. They usually come in boxes of six, and they should be kept in the box; if stored loose, they become shiny and do not take spin as well as new ones. Store them away from heat, which embrittles them.

NETS AND POSTS

These are seldom available locally. A net should be suspended six inches high by a single cord running through the upper binding; any other suspension (or even this one if loose) will introduce too much luck by dropping net-balls too close. The net must be six feet long,

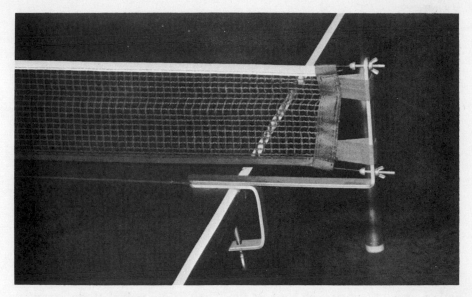

Figure 31—The Extension of the Net

projecting six inches beyond each side of the table (Figure 31). Most nets purchased locally are shorter than this and have no cord. A good set costs about $4.

TABLES

Look for the seal of approval. The dimensions of the table are given in Figure 1. The top is preferably 3/4 inch thick. Excellent plywood tops are available, but some have "dead" spots. Particle-board tops are more certain to be uniform.

If the table is to remain in one place permanently, an eight-leg model, costing $40-$60, should be obtained. If it must be stored after each use, secure a roll-away model. These cost $60-$150, but the added durability is well worth the investment. An eight-leg model usually has chipped edges when it has been moved a few times; if you must move one, store the halves vertically with the faces together, resting on the net edges.

The playing surface should be lightly dusted occasionally with a damp cloth. Do *not* dust heavily or wax; the last thing desired is a shiny table. If you treat your table well, and use it only for table tennis, it will provide years of service.

EQUIPMENT

RACKETS

Good rackets (p. 5) are occasionally available locally, but there is seldom much variety. A good one costs about five dollars and may be purchased from a club or from one of the dealers who advertise in the USTTA magazine. Keep your racket away from heat; excess heat will damage the rubber. Clean inverted sandwich occasionally with a damp sponge.

LIGHTING

Even a poor player senses an inadequacy if the light intensity is less than twenty foot-candles at the playing surface; the tournament minimum is thirty foot-candles. Your local power company will be glad to measure the intensity for you and will also suggest how to obtain any desired intensity.

FLOOR

You may have little control over the floor. It is preferably resilient and of wood. (Concrete is hard on the feet.) Use a non-skid, dull wax.

SHOES

These, like socks, are preferably white. For gripping slippery floors, the slight premium paid for boat shoes is well justified. These are washable in home laundries.

OTHER CLOTHING

The upper and lower garments must be of dark, solid colors. Shirts should be short-sleeved, preferably with a button or zip neck. If open necked be sure that the undershirt is covered. Dark, solid-colored shirts are surprisingly hard to find. Decorative piping, which is not permitted, is in vogue. If your search is unrewarded, write to the USTTA. Shorts are even more difficult to find. Gym types are satisfactory if not too short, too shiny, or multi-colored. The USTTA can provide addresses of manufacturers who supply table tennis shorts; the same companies also handle skirts, which are of skating length.

For keeping warm between matches, a sweat suit or track suit is more comfortable than slacks and sweaters. Although some officials frown on it, a few players prefer to play the first game of a match wearing their warm-up suit, which must therefore be of a legal color. The USTTA can provide addresses of companies selling suitable warm-up suits.

Playing the Game

With your new-found skills, you will want to practice and to compete in a table tennis club if there is one in your area. This book, however, is directed primarily toward college students. What follows offers some methods of maintaining interest within your college.

There are several types of singles or doubles tournaments which could be conducted within a college and between colleges. These are described in the following sections.

SINGLE ELIMINATION (Knock-Out)

Almost everyone is familiar with this type; a draw is shown in Figure 32. Two points of difficulty are seeding and byes. The last match, or final, should be the best. The two strongest players, if known, are therefore put in the top positions of opposite halves of the draw; they are indicated in the draw by *s*. Usually one player in every eight is thus seeded. For example, if there are about 32 players you will seed four, the extra two being given (by lot) the top positions in the remaining quarters.

If the number of entries is not an integral power of two, then some receive byes (see page 57). The number of byes is the difference between the number of players and the next highest power of two. Seeded players, in order, have the first byes, any extras being distributed evenly.

GROUP ROUND ROBIN

In a round-robin event, everyone plays everyone else. If there are too many players, divide them into smaller round robins. (Figure 33).

SELECTED REFERENCES

1962   Barna, Victor. *Table Tennis Today.* London: Sir Isaac Pitman & Sons, Ltd., 1962. Interesting appendix contains biographies of many of the great players, seen through the eyes of the most successful of them all.

1965   Rowe, Diane. *Table Tennis.* London: Stanley Paul & Co., Ltd., 1965. Especially good for girls. Good chapters on tactics and training. Section on the penholder grip.

1966   Harrower, Geoffrey. *Table Tennis.* London: English Universities Press, 1966.

1967   Miles, Richard. *The Game of Table Tennis.* Philadelphia: J. B. Lippincott Company, 1967. In press.

FILMS

The USTTA can lend the following films to interested groups. All except the first listed are 16 mm. black and white with sound track.

Athletic Institute: *How to Improve Your Table Tennis.* 35mm. film strip, associated booklet, and phonograph record. For beginners.

Barna-Szabados: A fine demonstration of the pimpled-rubber game by two of the best.

Carrington: The coaching of beginners.

World Championships, Peking, 1961. Excellent topspin table tennis. Two reels.

World Championships, Stockholm, 1957. Largely sequences of the stars in action.

MAGAZINES

Canadian Table Tennis News. Publication of the Canadian association.

Table Tennis News. Excellent magazine; English association publication.

Table Tennis Topics. Official magazine in the United States, published nine times a year.

Tennis. Covers all racket sports; is published monthly; address is Box 5, Ravinia Station Highland Park, Illinois 60035.

For those interested in foreign language publications, three magazines worthy of attention are:

  BT (Sweden)

  Deutscher Tischtennis Sport (Germany)

  The Table Tennis Report (Japan)

Information on any of these magazines is available from the United States Table Tennis Association; for the address, see Gale's *Encyclopedia of Associations* in your local library.

71 572 358